Roshan and Roshina

ROSHAN B. KARKI

DEDICATION

To my beautiful wife Roshina
Travel forever with me

CONTENTS

Acknowledgments   i

1   Poems about Roshan and Roshina   3-18

2   Poems about love   19-38

3   Poems about roads, freedom   39-46

    and other subjects

4   Few Pictures   47-58

ACKNOWLEDGMENTS

POEMS ABOUT ROSHAN AND ROSHINA

A New Year's Eve

We will go to Thamel in New Year's Eve.
We will drink a bottle of wine sip by sip.
It's history of time to start a new year.
You are my love. You are my peer.

The history will remember knights and kings.
Will the history remember lovers I wonder?
The moon is on the height. The couples are in the
street.
Don't waste the night. Dance to the beat.

Here in Thamel nightlife is folklore.
Tomorrow will be brand new day and brand new
year.
Let's not waste the night by being sober.
Kiss and hug your peer.

Be my baby, be by Bride

See the lights
Make me feel alive
I am by your side
It's a beautiful night

Let the lights shimmer
Let your heart glitter
I will always be by your side
Be my baby, be my bride.

You give me a reason to keep going
May be god created you
Make you forever mine
Be by baby, be my bride.

Dating Roshina

We met sober in a restaurant
in New Baneshwor.
You looked beautiful.
The table was full of roses.

You ordered a cappuccino
I ordered a mocha
I secretly took your picture
and mailed it to my father.

We talked and talked
until there was nothing left to talk.
We watched the sun sleep
somewhere in the sea shore.

We have long way to go
and this is only beginning.
We will walk slowly with love.
Beautiful are my feelings.

Down in Downtown

I will wait for you at Frisco's bar
like I always have.
Come to meet me for a drink. It's not very far.
It's Friday. I am down in downtown.

I will put you in my car.
Friday nights are interesting here.
We will drink merlot and beer
and roll down in downtown.

Get ready for a drink and date.
I will wait for you like I always have.
Do me a favor do not be late.
We will roll down to downtown.

Garden of love

I was walking with Roshina
when we passed the garden of love.
The lovers were kissing.
We asked each other, "Should we stop?"

We asked for a pass.
The receptionist said, "Only couples
with pure love are welcome here."

So we measured our love.
We found no selfishness there.
The receptionist said, "You are welcome here.
You can spend thousands of lives here."

There were red roses.
There was blue jasmine.
There was wine
and smell of divine fragrance.

The sun and the moon rose together
as couples in garden of love.
We felt we more near
when we rested on garden of love.

So we waited for the night.
The stars were shimmering in the sky.
The sun and the moon went to sleep

in the divine cosmos bed.

Our love was much.
Our heart glittered like diamonds.
No watch can measure love
in the green garden of love.

Get lost with you

I want to get lost with you
deep in jungle, deep in night
when you are by my side.
We will pass the whole life
looking for a way out.
A path we will never find
I will never leave you behind
as long as you are mine.
We will look at roses and Jasmine.
The stars will glitter. The moon will shine.
We will never find a way out
but we will find each other.
That will end the motto of life.
Our love is high like Himalayas.
We will thus find the aim of life.
We will talk together sleepless in the nights.
God from heaven will bless us from height.
We will thus find the motto of life.

Heights of the World

Join your hands with me
Kiss me deep in sleep
Be with me forever and
I will take you to the heights of the world.

I will take you to power,
riches and fame.
Do not just close that door and
I will take you to heights of the world.

And we will do it together
You and me
Hope is more valuable than anything ever.
I will take you to the heights of the world

Let's start the Day Together

You broom the room
When I am deep in sleep
dreaming about you because
you are so sensual.

You cook rice and
I will prepare vegetables.
The sun is about to wake
In co-operation the world lays

Now, we should hurry down to work.
You stay with me for five minutes more.
The morning with you is just like folklore
when we start the day together.

Roshan and Roshina

The two formed a pair in heaven and
walked on earth to prove it.
They were born among dark forests.
Life was an adventure to them. They nailed it.

Life was a motto to them
A walk to find each other
Many time they failed
but kings of heaven did not like it.

As they were formed in heaven
nothing could separate them.
Soon life took their tests and
both passed on it

These days they are together
Gods are happy for it.
They formed a pair in heaven
and walked on earth to prove it.

They kiss each other
and support each other if the day is their last.
Life is a present of Gods
and in it they will make a blast.

Roshina, let me sing for you

Roshina, let me sing for you
It is a Friday night
Few lovers are on street
The streets are silent and quiet.

Let me feel you are mine
if so the music will feel divine.
We have whole night to live
It's only nine.

You will get entertained
I will feel divine
The bliss of love is in whole room
It's just half past ten.

And in bed
Let me dream about you
Let me feel purity of heaven
Let the gloomy moon be happier
The streets are cold. We will shiver.

Roshina, travel forever with me

You are in light and in the night.
You are my everything. I owe you my life.
Despite the waves and tides in the sea
Roshina, travel forever with me

You are beautiful in day and romantic in night.
Your glimpse in my eyes will never fade away.
Despite the troubles, pain and tides in the sea
ignore them Roshina. Travel forever with me.

Roshina

You are everywhere
from pulse to heartbeat.
I need you like I need air.
You have made my life so clear.

Your every kiss and touch
Gives me a reason to live
A reason to keep going
You are my greatest friend.

From dusk to dawn
I forever remain to your name
I love you like nothing
The sun and the moon will feel ashamed.

Day by day our love will increase
It will grow exponentially
I am proud
to be tied to your name.

16

Shopping Together

The mall is far
I do not have car
The sky is full of stars
We are drinking coffee in a bar
My card has fifty dollars.
We will visit the mall and beauty parlor as
today you are my girl.
and we will do shopping together.

Sweet as Chocolate

You are sizzling in rain.
You are sensible to pain.
Let the sun rise with your beauty.
Just like the moon you will be never lonely.
Let the stars hover above your hair.
Let your zodiac constellation bless you forever.
Your lips are as red as roses.
Let your heart be room which never closes.
Let God bless our life.
You are by buddy. You are my mate.
Roshina, you are sweet as chocolate.

The Princess Yesterday, Now is my Bride

The princess yesterday is now my bride
She is sleeping by my side
Listen to the calm sea in the night
From today you are forever mine.

Let the doves fly high in the sky
Kiss me deep. Do not feel shy.
In the bliss of love the whole world lays.
You were princess yesterday, now you are my bride.

Our marriage is vow to be together
From this day for forever and ever
We will reincarnate thousands of life
You were princess yesterday, now you are my bride.

POEMS ABOUT LOVE

A Paradise

I want to dip
in ocean of your eyes
and count the number of times
you have seen me kissing you.

Your serene eyes
in the garden of our love,
the love of our paradise
makes me feel you are forever mine.

And together we will travel
down the road
filled with snow
and we will count the number of times
our foot prints have covered the beach.

We will make earth a paradise.

Beautiful Moments

Let us treasure
our beautiful moments.
Love is more expensive
then trillions of cents.

Going out is just a way
In our love the whole world lay
We will grow old together.
Our treasures are our beautiful moments.

Let us visit discotheques and bars.
Life is more fun when death is not very far.
Three decades and I finally found you.
Our beautiful moments will last for thousands of
years.

Fire and Champagne

Welcome the night with fire and champagne.
The moon in glittering so is your ring.
Let's not waste a single second.
You are my partner. You are my friend.

Let the night glow with lust and love.
The night is here but do not hurry up.
Welcome the hours with fire and champagne.
You are mine. You are tied to my name.

Put more woods. Let the hours be swift.
Love is a religion. Our life is a gift.
Do not waste a single second.
Welcome the night with fire and champagne

If (modified from "If" by Rudyard Kipling)

If you walk on the street with your pair
despite criticism, thorns and despair
If you can keep your trust when people doubt you,
But make allowances for doubting to.

If you can wait her in park and not be tired of waiting
Or never lie to her, don't deal in lies,
Or being neglected, do not give a damn about it,
And look good, walk with her:

If you can kiss-
And not make tragedy your master;
If you can think-
And not make thoughts your aim;

If you can meet with challenges and pain
And treat those imposters just the same;
Yours is the earth and everything that's in it,
And my couples, you will be queen and king

Let the Party Begin

Tik tok. Tik tok. It's ten.
Let the party begin
I am drinking champagne
cheering to your name.

It's Friday
and half past ten.
Let me ease your pain
with this fine champagne.

Let me count the number of stars and
make me feel I am in paradise.
Let me grow wings like a kite.
Let the party begin

I feel I just won the world
with this glass of champagne.
Tik tok. Tik tok. It's ten.
Let the party begin.

24

Let us live

Let us live and make merry
Let us create wonderful story
Though life is fast do not hurry
Walk in the park. Book a ferry.

Let us live and make merry
Down in discotheques and bars
Let them dream about roses
Let them glance as the stars.

Create a wonderful love story as
we walk in earth with love and care.
Don't hide your love. Please share it.
Without love the world will go numb and bare

Love and Heroes

Krishna had Radha.
Shiva has Parvati.
Napoleon Bonaparte had Josephine.
I have Roshina.

Love is a strong stimulant as
it saves the world.
It brings best of men
out in the world.

This desire to please a woman
passes from human to human.
A dark box of wonder waits
to those who please woman.

From a zero
You will be a hero
Love is a great stimulant as
it brings out best of men.

Love and Money

Love is expensive
Money is cheap
Love is like a ocean
and money is its fleet of ship.

Some say love does not cost money
but money makes life better.
Being in love is being a billionaire
but clubs and bar charges fair.
You need money to buy wine and beer

Money brings best of love
Go to bars, discotheques and anywhere
You need solid dollars
for love to maintain here.

Love and Politics

What's the difference between love and politics?
Both are game of life. It's a play if genius.
In love there are princess and prince.
In politics there are kings and beggars.

What's the difference between love and politics?
Roses grow in garden. Swords are made for thunder.
Let's add a little politics to our love, a little trick.
What will it bring in the world I wonder?

But politics well played creates more lovers.
It will make new homes, food and shelter.
Love is an expression. Politics is a game.
Drink a glass of wine cheering to your lover's name.

Love is a Vision, Death is a Tragedy

Some visions rule down the earth
and fill the interspaces of the Universe.
Between the two pure hearts love lies.
Love is a vision, death is a tragedy.

May everyone live for hundreds of years
May everyone be blissful with feelings of love
Between the heaven and hell this world lay
Love is a vision, death is a tragedy.

May there be no calamities and no wars
Hate is small. Boundary of love is large.
Between heaven and hell the world lies.
Love is a vision, death is a tragedy.

Love is all we have

I will make you secure and content
because love is all we have.
Life can be a way to heaven
and to constellations and stars.

Let your ring glitter. Show it with pride.
We will watch the sun go down.
We will watch the moon and tides.

Love creates more love
War creates more war
Love is a journey
to heaven, constellation and stars.

Some love stories never end

Some love stories never end.
They will inspire loners to find a friend.
They will remain in history despite the pain.
Love can heal even if reality is insane.

Some love stories never end as
down in the book of history they will remain.
To the cosmos and universe it will spread.
Love is a divinity. It can only be felt.

Some Money

If you have some money to give
do not give it to beggars.
Give it to newly married couples.
They will go the discotheques and bars.
They will live
despite money beggar will continue to beg.

The Divine Love

Hear Krishna play harmonious flute and
Radha listen to it in woods.
Here love is sign of divinity.
There is less masculinity and more femininity.
This world and total cosmos surrender to their divine
love.

The Island of Love

Here in island of love
It's fairytale
Everyone has a pair as
we do not welcome the loner's here.

You hold my hand
and put a ring.
You kiss your lover
You dance and sing

You talk and talk
about stars and love.
You believe in love
You believe in luck

Island of love lies
deep in your heart.
There is no way out and
entry if you are made of love

Never smoother the island
Make it beautiful with your presence
Make love and spread the divine fragrance.

34

The Joy of rowing together

The river is calm and sober
when we are rowing down together.
Our love will last forever,
deep in the night we are rowing down the river.

In luxury of love I might suffer from fever.
I will keep you warm. We will never shiver.
down while we are rowing down the river.
Day by day the river is getting stranger

Only love can bind us together
The River of life is very clever.
With each year's we will get braver
because we are rowing down in an endless river.

The World needs More Lovers

The world does not need more missiles.
It needs more lovers.
It needs more pair of doves in the sky.
Keep love in heart despite troubles.

The world need not more guns.
It needs humanity in hearts of men.
It needs more fables and tales
like the story of Romeo and Juliet.

Love has place in heaven
If there the ten million pairs
nothing can destroy the world
despite wars, despair and pain.

Walk on the Beach

It's late in night
We are in beach watching the tides
The moon is on the sky
We will walk on the beach together.

May be the waves will erase
our footprints on the beach.
Let the magic of life unleash
Start the enigma with your kiss.

You are hot and so is the shore.
We are watching the waves since four.
Look the moon is on the sight.
We will walk on the beach together.

You are my Symphony

You are my symphony
You are my metaphor
You are my warmth from inside
when you are by my side.

You are my ocean
Your lips are mine
When you are by my side
we will overcome the tides.

You brighten my day
you are stars at night
Oh dear! Time passes smooth
when you are by my side.

You are my life
You are colors of night
You are love of my life
You are love of my life.

You are my Universe

Love is a form of god.
You are my world
Your eyes shimmer like stars
You are my metaphor
Only language I understand
Our relationship is eternity
You are my love
You are my universe

POEMS ABOUT ROADS, FREEDOM AND OTHER SUBJECTS

A Hymn to US Military

If we win the earth will be heaven.
If we lose we will go to heaven.
My love if you lost me
think you lost a hero who took earth to a better path.

Birds

May be the birds think human world
is chained to sky
when they are way high up and
they are looking down.

May be birds have their own languages.
They have their own metaphors and similes.
They have own kings, queens and beggars
but they too are chained to the sky.

Free the birds in the cage.
Be a freedom fighter, be a sage.
Let the birds fly up high
but they too are chained to the sky.

Goddess Saraswoti

Your letters made in heaven
gave me power to get dreams.
It motivated me to go further
when I was in nursery class.

Soon I learned
you are in poetry and philosophy.
I devoured all of Dante's poetry
to get a glimpse of you.

Then I learned you are in books.
I started writing novels and
with each word
I feel I am closer to you.

And with each hour
with every thought I am thinking
I felt I am becoming you.

Learning to Live

I met an old man down by street.
I asked, "Old man what you are doing?"
He said, "I am in my eighties
I am learning to live again."

Lost in the Woods

I got myself to lost in the woods
I wanted to think alone for who I am
and in way the trees stood
just like me not knowing about themselves.

Someday I have to go deep in the cities.
I got to clarify what my role is.
I wanted to find the way for this selfish world.
I got to do as God's of heaven has told.

Let me make nature my friend.
Let me walk for a mile and more as
where peace in the world lies is strange
because my years in number is four decades and four.

Let me forget my possessions for a while.
Let me make nature my friend.
Let me listen to folklore of wind because
life and death is a cycle. It is a trend.

Meaningless Roads

Where does the road go? I do not know.
It's cold and the ground is covered with snow.
Only way out is to walk along
down the ways of meaningless roads.

Until there is life there is hope.
A beggar might be king. A commoner might be pope.
So walk carefully until the end of the road as
life is hard so is the road.

You may feel hot. You may feel cold
down the path of meaningless roads.
The best thing is to walk with partner.
It will make life meaningful, avoid disasters.

The Art of Love

Firstly, praise here as if she is a flower.
Be with her every hour.
She is a gift from heaven.
Love is a gift and it is a power.

Secondly, see eternity in love and
take her to bars and clubs.
Kiss her deep in the nights,
see the dawn and see the twilight.

Thirdly, help her in household works
Love lies deep in support.
Work together to clean, dust and broom.
The love then will grow exponentially.

The Dancers

We all are dancing in the dark
between every sunrise and sunset.
The god above is playing dice and
we dance to his guitar.

None knows what happens after death.
He gives his visions when we are in bed.
Between hell and heaven this world lay.
There are dues in life we must pay.

So be cheerful why are you sad?
Has the creator above gone mad?
Between every sunrise and sunset
we dance to tunes of his guitar.

FEW PICTURES

(ROSHINA AS A BRIDE)

(ROSHAN AND ROSHINA AT MARRIAGE)

(ROSHINA AT MARRIAGE)

(ROSHAN AND ROSHINA AT A RESTAURANT)

(ROSHAN AND ROSHINA AT A CLUB)

(ROSHAN AND ROSHINA AT PICNIC)

(ROSHAN AND ROSHINA AT THEIR ANNIVERSARY)

(ROSHAN AND ROSHINA AT NAGARKOT)

(ROSHAN AND ROSHINA AT MYSIC MOUNTAIN
RESORT NAGARKOT)

(ROSHAN AND ROSHINA CELEBRATING NEW YEAR'S EVE)

(ROSHAN AND ROSHINA CELEBRATING ROSHAN'S
BIRTHDAY)

58

(ROSHAN AND ROSHINA AT A B

ABOUT THE AUTHOR

Roshan B. Karki (Roshan Bikram Kark) is a poet, writer, musician and entrepreneur. He was born in Charikot, Dolkha. He has attended Loras College, USA as a honors student to pursue undergraduate in Creative writing. " Roshan and Roshina" is twelveth book by the author. Written about pure love experiences it consists of love themes of the pair.